Astral Projection

A beginner's guide to astral travel and having an out-of-body experience

Lauren Lingard

Table of Contents

Introduction 1

Chapter One: What is Astral Projection 3

Chapter Two: The History of Astral Projection Across Different Cultures..7

Chapter Three: What Astral Travel Can Be Used For 11

Chapter Four: Other Tools to help you project 17

Chapter Five: How to Try Astral Travel Yourself 25

Chapter Six: How to Stay Safe while Trying Astral Projection........34

Chapter Seven: What to Do if You're Having Trouble Projecting ...38

Chapter Eight: What happens next? Expanding on what you've learned 44

Chapter Nine: Lucid Dreaming 57

Final Words 60

Introduction

At the end of the day, Mia lies down to go to sleep. She's done everything the experts suggest: she rode her bike, she took a hot bath, and she turned off the television early, but after a long day at work, her thoughts are still racing.

She's tried meditating, but it didn't click. She's tried breathing exercises, but it didn't quiet her mind. She even tried drinking a glass of red wine, but that just made her feel even more awake. Is there anything else she can do?

Yes! There is another way.

Mia can escape the perils of her day, and engage her mind, all thanks to a technique called astral projection.

Mia gets up and stretches her shoulders out, and then she lies back down, remembering the book she read about astral projection a few days before. She recalls the steps and gives it her best effort. At first, she can't stay focused. But after three tries, she is pretty sure she feels her conscious mind pull away from her body.

It works! She floats, inches above her body, marveling at the different perspective. She moves forward a little bit to see the side view of her ceiling fan. Outside, car tires screech, but it all feels very far away from her. It doesn't affect her placid state.

Then her phone buzzes, and she's pulled back into the real world.

But she feels different.

She feels lighter, and suddenly sleep no longer seems so far away. She can't remember what she was worried about at all, and, sighing happily, she drifts off into a tranquil sleep.

Why would anyone *want* to try astral projection?

There are quite a few reasons for anyone to give it a shot. On a very basic level, there are benefits that can include more energy, less stress and tension, a sense of peace, and a newfound interest in everyday life.

There are other benefits too, such as an increased interest in spirituality or religion. Some people have reported healing taking place in their physical bodies while their mind was on the astral plane. And others have reported discovering a new way to look at death and the afterlife.

Or for some people, it can be a way to break away from the demands of the world, just like Mia did.

There are plenty of books and websites that will jump right into advanced astral projection ideas with talk of spirit guides, past lives, and future reincarnation, and we will get into those quite compelling topics later. But this book is going to start with the basics, and give real, concrete steps to follow, so that if you're ever feeling a little bummed about your progress, you can come right back to the recommendations listed here and try again.

As you read this guide, keep in mind that astral projection is a skill, just like cooking or painting. It takes time and practice, and it may not happen on the first try. But if you use the methods in this book, you're well on your way to your first successful astral projection!

Chapter One: What is Astral Projection

What is astral projection?

If you're new to the topic, you may be wondering exactly what the term means. It *does* sound a little bit complicated, but the simplest explanation is that it is something that happens when your spirit leaves your physical body behind for a short period of time.

Once you've left your physical body behind, then your spirit is free.

Free to explore, to fly, to meet other spirits, and visit worlds you may have only imagined before. But we'll get to that part later on.

The astral part of the term comes from the idea that we all have a physical body and an astral body. You know what the physical body is — that's the part of you we can see and touch.

The astral body is the part of ourselves that's not tangible. It's composed of our spirit, or our soul, and some practitioners refer to it as our 'light body' or our 'subtle body'.

Just as the physical world exists, made up of cars, and streets and buildings, the astral world exists too and so when we leave our physical body and enter the astral plane, we are projecting our body into that invisible world.

So astral projection is the art of pulling our conscious mind out of our body and entering another world. It can feel just like dreaming, but the big difference is that you're wide awake.

Your astral body isn't tied to the rules of gravity, like your physical body is. You may even be able to float above your body and look down on it from above.

That sounds pretty cool, right?

Experienced practitioners agree that it's a pretty incredible experience, especially when it's planned. However, there are other ways that the mind can leave the body. Not all of them are on purpose. Astral projection is just one type of an out of body experience (OBE).

An OBE takes place when the mind separates from the body, but it might not always be something the person wanted, sometimes it can even be something terrifying. Sometimes an OBE can happen without it being an intentional choice, such as a traumatic event or a near death experience. It can also happen through the use of chemical substances, or while dreaming.

But for the purposes of this book, we'll concentrate most of our time on the intentional separation of the body from the conscious mind, which is called astral projection.

But is it Real?

A common question beginners will ask is, 'is astral projection real? Can your mind really leave your body?' Experienced practitioners will give you an absolute *yes* as an answer.

Astral projection, though, is a personal experience, unique to each of us, just as our dreams are unique. Your dreams are real, and yet no one else can experience them with you.

The same is true of your spirituality. And you will discover that your projections fit into that category as well.

You may also be wondering what the scientific community has to say about it?

Because astral projection is such a personal experience, it differs for most people. But there has been some interesting research conducted.

On February 10, 2014, the *Frontiers of Human Neuroscience* published a paper called *Voluntary out-of-body-experience: an fMRI study*. (The fMRI stands for functional magnetic resonance imaging, which is a machine that measures the blood flow in the brain.)

Scientists used the fMRI machine to observe a volunteer subject's brain while she practiced astral projection. The volunteer was a psychology student from the University of Ottawa who claimed she'd been practicing astral projection all of her life, without knowing there was even a name for it. When she mentioned that fact to her professor, he was intrigued, and wanted to study her brain waves.

The brain changes noted in that scan were consistent with the movements that she was making with her astral body, all while her physical body was lying still.

The study is fascinating, but even without it, it is clear that astral projection is a real phenomenon that millions of people have experimented with for thousands of years.

And the good news is, you don't need scientific proof to believe in astral projection, you just need faith that it works, that other people do it and you can learn how. The best way to answer the question of 'is it real?' is to try it for yourself. This book will help you figure out the way that works for you.

As you read, keep in mind that astral projection is an individual experience. You may hover gently above your body, staying in your own bedroom. Or you may end up being able to fly through the world, or even the universe!

Both experiences are valid, and both have immense benefits for us as human beings. One other word of caution: you will probably be really excited about your success at some point, and you'll want to share everything you know with your friends and family. That part can be fun, but don't get discouraged if they aren't interested. Give them time.

They will likely see the positive changes in your life, and then ask how you made them happen.

Also, when you've been projecting for a while, you may come to feel that much of the mundane stuff we obsess about in the physical world is fairly insignificant. Sometimes it can be difficult to watch people we're close to bicker over petty issues, especially when we know they'd be happier and more serene if they'd only open their minds and listen to us.

However, it's probably best to keep these thoughts to yourself, or only share them with a close friend who understands your new point of view. You won't win over any converts to astral travel if you tell them how juvenile and irritating their views on the world are!

Chapter Summary

- In this chapter we learned the definition of astral travel. The simplest definition is that astral travel takes place when the mind separates from the body.

- We touched on how science views astral travel, including the use of a study with brain imaging during a volunteer's journey to the astral plane.

In the next chapter you will learn about the history of astral travel across the world, and how it's become a part of popular culture, through books, television, and movies.

Chapter Two: The History of Astral Projection Across Different Cultures

Astral projection is a very *old* practice; it's been in use for thousands of years. Some ancient cultures documented their beliefs in great detail, and many of those ideas were the same across widely differing cultures.

Even today, in modern times, the practices we use may be quite similar to those methods used thousands of years ago.

The ancient Egyptians were one of the first cultures to describe astral projection. They believed the soul was made up of five separate parts. The 'Ka' was considered the spirit, or vital essence. The Egyptians believed the Ka could leave the body and travel.

In ancient China, the Taoists had a practice which involved breathing meditations, which allowed the inner spirit to travel to other places.

Plutarch, a historian in ancient Greece, tells a story of a man who fell and hit his head. While he was unconscious, the man had an involuntary OBE. Plutarch's description of the experience is similar in what he describes to the examples we can find in modern society.

The Hindu religion has a rich history of knowledge about astral travel. It says that Siddhis - the Sanskrit word for 'magical' powers - can be gained through specific meditations and Yoga exercises. The Bhagavata Purana, one of the ancient yogi texts, mentions the ability to use astral travel.

Tantric Buddhism has relied on astral projection as a central tenet for thousands of years.

And according to some scholars, in 2 Corinthians 12:1–4 of the Christian Bible, the apostle Paul refers to a man who experiences an OBE, by saying he was 'caught up to the third heaven.'

Native Americans used a flute to play trance-inducing music that was said to aid astral travel, and in Central America, a powerful plant brew called *ayahuasca* has been traditionally used by shamans to induce an out of body experience.

The brew comes from a plant that is called 'soul vine' or 'vine of the dead.' It has been used in their healing ceremonies by indigenous groups in Bolivia, Brazil, Colombia, Ecuador, and Peru, and there is evidence that it has been in use since 905 AD.

So, as you can see, astral travel isn't a new phenomenon. In 1978, sociologist Dean Sheils writing in the *Journal of the Society for Psychical Research*, reported that of the sixty cultures that had been studied, fifty-four had had some kind of belief in astral travel.

Astral Projection in Popular Culture

Astral projection doesn't just exist in history books or 'how-to' instructional manuals. It's a topic that has shown up in media and popular culture across the world, for the last several decades.

Games

In the popular tabletop role-playing game, *Dungeons & Dragons,* astral projection was one of the many options a player could use on their turn. The astral projection spell in the game was much like it is in real life. It allowed the player's character to travel in the astral plane, while leaving his or her body behind in an unconscious state.

Books

In Italy in 1308, Dante Alighieri began writing his narrative poem, *Divine Comedy*. In his work, he creates a fictional version of himself that travels to heaven and hell. His poem came to signify the Western version of the afterlife.

In *Through her Eyes,* a 2017 novel by Sarah Pinborough, the main character quickly masters astral travel, to the point of being able to take over someone else's body. The book was later adapted to a Netflix show.

Television and Movies

Although fun to watch, some of the depictions in popular television shows and movies are for entertainment only, and they do not represent the truth.

In the popular horror movie *Insidious*, the main character is caught up in a nightmarish scenario that features astral projection. But not all of the representations are as scary to watch.

The Twilight Zone featured a show about astral travel in 1963, called *The Ring a Ding Girl*. By projecting herself, the main character ends up saving her friends and family from a plane crash.

In the Marvel Cinematic Universe movie, *Doctor Strange*, Stephen Strange learns to project himself around the world, and even to other universes and dimensions.

It can be fun to enjoy these shows, but remember that they have been made for entertainment, and are not 'how-to' guides. Don't let the ideas from these shows dissuade you from trying astral projection.

Chapter Summary

- Astral travel isn't new. It's an ancient practice; people have been practicing astral projection for more than a thousand years.

- Popular culture likes to distort the reality of astral projection for entertainment, by making it seem scary. But in reality, the practice is quite safe, and offers huge rewards for anyone who masters it.

In the next chapter, we'll learn what astral travel can be used for.

Chapter Three: What Astral Travel Can Be Used For

There are quite a few compelling reasons to try astral travel. And it makes sense to think about why it is that *you* want to learn this practice. You may have one reason, or you may have twelve. Or you may have heard about it on a podcast, and you're just curious. That's okay too. Below are some of the more common reasons people have worked hard to learn this skill.

Conquering a fear of dying

As mentioned in the introduction, one benefit cited over and over by practitioners is they become less afraid of death and dying. Many people across the world are terrified to think about what happens when their life ends. This all-encompassing fear can be crippling and can even keep them from living life to the fullest.

When a person learns to use astral travel, we learn that our spirits aren't connected to our bodies, and that means that moving on to the afterlife doesn't have to be a traumatic process.

Smooth transition to the afterlife

Hospice doctors, nurses, and social workers all work hard to make a patient's transition from life to death a little easier on both the patient and family members. When someone is told the end of their life is near, he or she may panic. But there are some methods that have been shown to ease this transition and even if the person is not an astral traveler themselves, there are still some techniques that can be used to help them face the end of their life.

William Buhlman has been practicing astral projection for forty years. In his manual, *Destination: Higher Self*, he recommends talking to a loved one who is dying about their spiritual nature. He says we can help guide them through the transition by being at their bedside and by reassuring them, and encouraging them to let go of their fear and attachment to their physical body.

Stress Relief

Many astral projection practitioners report intense feelings of relief after astral projection, similar to the kind of feelings of wellbeing that you'd experience after leaving a sauna, hot tub, or a relaxing massage. It may even feel like having a glass of wine, but the bonus is that there are no side effects or downsides to astral projection.

For many people, there are so many rules and restrictions in life, that inhabiting a world (the astral world) where there are no limits feels very freeing. They find that their blood pressure is lower, and their stress headaches are gone. Their entire body feels relaxed, and their muscles feel looser and less tense.

Spiritual Awakening

As you practice astral projection and become more experienced, you may feel a connection to a higher power. For some people, that means a continuation of their religion or an existing faith; for others, it's a new awareness that there's more to life than can be seen or touched. Some practitioners have reported an overall increased intuition while in the physical world.

Religious beliefs or faith in God is not a prerequisite to projecting though. Many people who are not religious have found a sense of profound spiritual enlightenment and a broader understanding of humanity.

Religion and Faith

Many religions promote the idea of an afterlife after one's physical body is dead. And if you do observe a religion, you may find astral projection is a way to gain a closer relationship with God.

With astral travel, you can begin to experience the reality of what it really means for your consciousness to survive and live on without your body. You may also find your personal faith journey somewhat easier once you've mastered astral projection.

Physical and Emotional Healing

While out of their body, some people have experienced healing from physical wounds or illnesses. They spend their time in the astral plane concentrating specifically on the part of the body that needs healing, such as focusing on a broken bone or a pulled muscle.

People whose physical bodies are disabled report a liberating sense of freedom from being unencumbered by the limitations of their physical world. Others have used the practice to specifically address the emotional and psychological wounds or trauma they've experienced, similar to the kind they'd discuss in therapy.

However, astral projection is not a substitute for medical care, either mental or physical, so don't skip your visits with your doctor or therapist!

Freedom from unwelcome habits

Some practitioners have reported finding it easier to break bad habits and addictions, such as smoking, excessive drinking, or even something as mundane as biting their nails.

They credit this new-found ability to the increased personal awareness they gain through astral travel.

Hypnosis, of course, has been used to help break these types of habits in the past, but it appears astral travel can be just as effective, if not more so! If, for example, you are struggling with overeating, or eating food that is unhealthy for your body, imagine yourself only eating foods that nourish your body. Visualize this habit changing both in the physical world and in the astral.

When the time comes, you can also ask your spirit guide for assistance.

Increased creativity

Any of your creative pursuits may be fueled by your foray into astral projection. You may have bursts of productivity while painting, drawing, exercising, writing, crafting, sewing, dancing, singing… or any hobby you engage in after you learn to travel on the astral plane.

The creativity and productivity is not limited to hobbies; you may also become more productive at work.

Projection? Where exactly can I go?

Many first-time astral travelers want to know where they're going, and where they'll end up. In the beginning, though, you will probably stay inside your physical body.

You may feel like your arms are lifting up, only to snap back into your body once you try to 'separate' from your chest or torso. Or you may successfully sit up or even hover above your body on the astral plane.

Once you're out of your body, the world may have an ethereal look to it. It may be shimmery, or the air around you may have a hazy or foggy look to it.

Once you're comfortable in your indoor space, you can move your astral body outside. And once you've mastered that, there are no boundaries to where you can go.

Some practitioners have traveled the planet on the astral plane — some have been to outer space and even to other worlds. Some have mastered visiting other people who are also traveling in the astral plane. And a few experts claim to be able to visit the past.

Some astral travelers have reported traveling to other realities, and parallel universes. Once you've reached this level of astral travel, your mind will expand, and you'll come to see the human definition of time as an illusion. Other practitioners have been able to visit loved ones who have passed away.

One practitioner warns that people who have died may not be accessible immediately. They have their own lives and priorities in the afterlife. But many people are able to visit their friends and family who've passed on, and most of them find great comfort in their visits.

How long should I stay?

At first, you may only be able to stay for a few seconds or a few minutes. Eventually, you may be able to sustain a projection that lasts a few hours. As long as your physical body is in a safe place, there is no real limit on how long you stay.

What should I avoid?

Once you've progressed beyond the basics, make sure you avoid using projection as a way to observe people without their knowledge. If they're engaged in private behavior, don't look in on them. Just as you'd respect their privacy in the physical world, respect it while you're in the astral world.

However, there will be other people who are also traveling in the astral plane and these are people you can visit.

Chapter Summary

- There are multiple benefits to practicing astral projection, among them are stress relief, increased spirituality, and physical and emotional healing.

- We learned about all the amazing places we can travel to in the astral plane.

In the next chapter you will discover other tools that will help you master astral projection; these include meditation, binaural beats, and chanting.

Chapter Four: Other Tools to help you project

It is rare that someone who has never tried astral projection before is successful on their first attempt. That said, there are those rare few people who can project themselves at will, at any time, and from any location.

But that's not how it works for most of us. Most of us will need a little extra help getting started, and we may need some help getting in the right mindset too. Here, we'll discuss several techniques that will calm your mind and make your path to astral travel much easier.

Meditation is one of the main ways to get ourselves in the right mindset.

Meditation

For those who are interested, we're going to talk a little bit about meditation here, and not least because some practitioners consider astral projection a simply a more advanced type of meditation.

You'll definitely have heard of meditation; the word gets bandied around quite a bit in pop culture today, although sometimes, it is so overused people just roll their eyes when another person starts to extoll the wonders of meditation.

This is a shame because there is now a body of scientific research to support the claimed health benefits and even the medical community now knows meditation can help with anxiety, depression, PTSD, pain, and stress.

The goal here is not to convince you that meditation is the only way to become good at astral projection - because it's not. But there are some points about meditation that you should be aware of.

How it works

Brain waves come from electrical pulses in our brains; there are several different types, and all humans have them.

According to psychologists, the brains of people who have meditated extensively look different on scans than the brains of the rest of us. One of the distinct differences is the activity levels of a brainwave called gamma waves.

These are the brainwaves that are seen when a person is intensely focused on a task. We all have gamma waves, but for most of us, they usually appear as a short burst on a scan, and then disappear.

But the brains of people who meditate at an Olympic level show high levels of gamma brainwaves all the time, all day, every day.

Many experts seem to agree with this assessment and have referred to meditation as a workout for your brain. Again, being proficient at meditation is not a requirement for astral traveling, but it can help if you're stuck, or if you want to improve your ability to project.

Many practitioners claim meditation has made it easier for them to open their mind to the very idea of astral travel. Meditation can help slow your brain and each time you practice it, it gets easier. It's as if you're training your brain to learn to behave in a new way, which, in turn, makes it easier to visit the astral plane.

For many people, meditation is a flop, but they still find great success with astral travel. In fact, some people report feeling the same benefits from their astral projection sessions as others report after extensive meditation.

But it doesn't have to be all or nothing with meditation. There are several astral projection meditations that can work to help us achieve our goals.

One of them involves visualizing a ball of light to guide us out of our body. Others include binaural beats, guided hypnosis, and working with your chakras, all of which we will explain and explore in this guide, so don't worry if you haven't yet heard of these things.

Binaural beats

As we know, not everyone can plop down on the floor and enter a meditative state. But some of us, even those of us who really want to be able meditate, will need a little extra help. If traditional meditation methods don't appeal or work for you and/or you need help, then you may want to try using binaural beats.

If you haven't heard of them, binaural beats are simply soundwaves played at a certain frequency. Some scientists call them an auditory illusion.

What's interesting is that while you are passively listening to a binaural beat recording, your brainwaves will start to resemble the same brain waves of a person who is meditating; in other words, the beats actually change the pattern of your brain waves.

There are countless recordings of binaural beats on YouTube. Some people use them to help relieve anxiety, some use them as a sleep aid or to encourage creativity. Others use them to manage pain, but they can also be used to help us with astral projection. Of course, binaural beats won't send you off into the astral plane by themselves. You still have to put in effort with time and practice.

Chanting 'Om'

Even if you've never used it, you've probably heard of the word *'om'* before, even if only in television or movies.

You may have used it in a Yoga class, or in a guided meditation. It has three syllables, and is pronounced like *ah-oh-um*, or AUM. (There are plenty of free recordings available on the internet if you want to hear it for yourself.)

People use the *'om'* sound while meditating, because when the word is spoken, the vibration can be felt through your vocal cords and your chest. And while it is so closely linked with yoga, the usefulness of the *om* chant goes much further. It has even been shown to lower your blood pressure and improve your heart health too!

Scientists have spent quite a bit of time researching *'om'*. In October 2018, a study published in the *Asian Journal of Psychiatry* studied the changes chanting 'om' causes in the brain using MRIs to measure the brain waves in participants who chanted *'om'*, and comparing those changes to the brains of a control group who were just asked to make the *'sss'* sound.

The participants who chanted *'om'* experienced increased relaxation, and also had more positive changes in the autonomic nervous system.

When it comes to using *om* and chanting out loud, you may feel awkward at first. Many people say they feel silly, but it's free, and it's easy, and it may just help you on your path to astral projection! So, give it a try when you're alone, and you can see if it works for you.

Hypnosis

Hypnosis for astral projection is centered around the idea that since we don't have much control over our thoughts, they can intrude during our quest to achieve projection at the moment right when we've hit the vibrational stage. We could be nearly floating, and then our mind may start to wander.

Hypnosis is a powerful tool that helps us control our thoughts by accessing our subconscious mind. The subconscious part of our mind is the part which controls our dreams. It doesn't censor our thoughts and when we can access that part of our brain, we can enjoy increased focus and relaxation, but we also have increased suggestibility too.

We may feel like we're in a zoned-out trance, or like we're really sleepy. While some may treat hypnosis like a joke, hypnosis is a real tool used by therapists for treating anxiety and for doctors treating pain. It's also a great tool for astral travelers.

There are gifted practitioners who have built their careers offering hypnosis as a healing or self-development tool and you may choose to visit one. If you do, make sure he or she specializes in metaphysics or OBEs, instead of something unrelated to astral projection, such as weight-loss.

If you want to try self-hypnosis, there are numerous self-guided tutorials online. To explore self-hypnosis, you can find a script written out online.

Guided hypnosis can help you get into a trance-like state, which will aid in your attempts to project.

A note of caution: we've mentioned all the ways to get comfortable with astral projection, but we do need to add that you should never try projection, hypnosis, or meditation while driving a car, riding a motorcycle or a bicycle, or while operating any other type of vehicle. Even listening to a guided hypnosis session while driving could make you too relaxed, and not alert enough to pay attention to the road.

If you are a passenger on public transport, some of the exercises like deep breathing could be beneficial, but even then you would not want to go into a trance-like state. When we're in public, it's best to stay alert!

Deep breathing

How we breathe can affect our success at astral projection. Deep breathing is an important part of astral travel, simply because it can get your body in a relaxed state. Many of us breathe too quickly, or not deeply enough. So, if you can, take a minute now to become aware of the way you breathe.

Inhale very slowly through your nose, feeling your lungs inflate. Hold the breath for just a second and then very slowly, let the breath out of your mouth. Do this over and over, until it feels natural.

One special method called Box Breathing, or Four Square Breathing, has been used by Navy SEALS during high-stress missions. The method has been shown to help reduce panic.

To try it: inhale through your nostrils to the count of four. Hold that breath for four counts. Then exhale for a count of four.

Once you've exhaled your breath, hold it for another four counts. Then repeat.

If you need a little more guidance, there are plenty of YouTube videos online that will help you practice deep breathing techniques, including this one. Find the technique you like the best and it won't be long before you come to appreciate the way it feels to breathe this way, because this steady type of breathing affects every part of your body in a positive way.

Yoga

We all know yoga can help with weight loss and stress reduction, but it can also aid in your astral projection journey. During yoga, the combined effects of the deep breathing, the stretching, and the meditation together can lead to successful astral projections.

Yoga is a comprehensive health system that originated in India where it is also used to help with spiritual meditation. It teaches special postures that can also help you quiet your mind. When you perform the stretches, you're focusing on your breathing. You're also releasing the tension in your muscles, both of which can lead to a calmer mind.

Essential oils

Some practitioners use essential oils by dabbing them on the forehead, wrists, and back of the neck. They can aid in deeper breathing and relaxation. Some favorites for astral projection include frankincense, rosemary, jasmine, and cinnamon.

Outdoor practice

Go outside on a day when there's no wind, but there are white, puffy clouds in the sky. Don't try a traditional astral projection, but instead, lie on your back and stare up at the clouds.

First, imagine one spot on the cloud, and imagine poking a hole in it.

Next, imagine floating inside the cloud. Use your senses to take stock of how it feels, and how it smells. Try clapping your hands into the clouds. Imagine grabbing the cloud and kneading it like dough. Try stretching it out, then rolling it back up into a ball.

For some people, just being in proximity to nature can help them get closer to having the right mindset to project.

Lucid Dreaming

Lucid dreaming is another common method of getting closer to astral projection, but as it's not considered a way to calm your mind, we'll explore it in more depth in Chapter Nine.

Meditation, along with all of these tools, put you in control of your mind, which will get you closer to astral projection!

Chapter Summary

- There are numerous ways to calm the mind in preparation for astral travel. They include well-proven methods such as meditation, deep breathing, binaural beats, hypnosis, and yoga.

- Any one of these methods may be enough to achieve a quiet mind, or they may all be used together.

- In the next chapter you will learn the steps to try astral travel for yourself.

Chapter Five: How to Try Astral Travel Yourself

Astral projection is truly for everyone. All you need is a place to lie down, and some uninterrupted time.

You don't need money, or gadgets. You can be in great shape, or struggling with your health. You can be wealthy, or living on a shoe-string budget.

While reading, keep in mind that we humans are spiritual beings who inhabit a physical body. Even those who aren't convinced about astral travel will likely agree that we are so much more than just our bodies. Once we know and accept this then we should know too that there's a whole universe out there just waiting for us!

1. Choose the best time of day.

Some practitioners say morning is the best time, because you are less likely to fall asleep, and because they believe you need a clear separation between sleep and being awake. Many also believe that being rested will lead to the best outcome.

Early morning is also the time when you're the least likely to be interrupted by the outside world. But if you're more comfortable in the evening, then that's worth trying too. Using projection as a tool for quality sleep may not be your end goal, but it's definitely a worthy benefit.

If you are going to try astral traveling in the morning then some experts say get up, brush your teeth, drink some water, and eat a small snack before you begin. Then go to the place that you've chosen to try astral projection. Make sure that place is quiet, with no distractions. Others recommend starting as soon as you wake up, before the reality of the day can infringe on your mind. Some even think a half-awake state is beneficial.

Ultimately, you need to experiment, and see which way works best for you. If you fall back into a deep sleep, you'll know you need to make sure you're fully awake next time before starting.

Once you're ready to try astral projection, lie down on your back, or sit in a recliner if you're not comfortable lying flat. Put your legs out straight, and straighten your arms out to the sides, as opposed to crossing them.

Close your eyes, and do your best to keep them closed. If you have trouble keeping them closed, you can try a sleep mask for your first few attempts.

If your home is noisy, or there are ambient sounds like cars honking or dogs barking, you may want to use earplugs, or even try headphones. You can play white noise, or even some music without lyrics.

Sometimes a smaller room will work best, instead of a big open room, but everyone is different. If you're lying down, try pointing your head toward the north. You may prefer to try it when the sun is not streaming in the window, simply because we associate sunlight with getting up and moving.

2. Clear your mind.

We all know this is not easy; and that clearing your mind is easier said than done, especially during times of stress or crisis. It takes practice, and a lot of discipline.

Some practitioners always use meditation to help calm their minds and as we saw in the last chapter, meditation really can aid in your journey to astral projection.

Breathing deeply will help clear your mind too. Go back to the exercises in the last chapter and make sure each breath you take is deep and slow. Focus on a slow inhale and exhale until it begins to feel more natural to breathe this way.

Next, relax all of your muscles. Start with your toes, and put your focus on each individual body part, as you move up through your body all the way up to your head. Be aware of each muscle, and any tension it might be holding.

Now that your mind is clear and your body is relaxed, we can move on to the more exciting part.

3. Feel the vibrations

Once your breathing is even, and your body is fully relaxed, you should start to hear and feel vibrations. Just let it happen and acknowledge the vibrations. Don't rush through this stage either. Spend a few moments letting the vibrations wash through your entire body.

Once the vibrations strengthen, you will feel like you're in a trance.

It's worth noting though that, at first, it may not feel like a vibration to you. It feels differently to everyone. You might feel fuzzy, or heavier, or even lighter.

When you get to this point - it's worth celebrating!

This stage is crucial, and it's where many people get stuck. When you reach this point, take a moment to acknowledge how far you've come.

But then get back to focusing on the way your body feels, and what your mind is doing.

4. Choose a technique

There are a few ways to project. Like everything else mentioned, you may have to try out several of them to pick which ones work best for you.

With any technique, you may feel dizzy. Or you may feel like your body is tingling. The most common feeling is one of floating, but you may feel something entirely different, like sinking or buzzing. Don't worry. All of these feelings are normal.

Visualization: Visualization involves imagining an object as your astral body leaves your physical one.

Once you're comfortable with the vibrations you're feeling, open your eyes and pick out a physical object, such as a vase on your dresser. Direct your focus to that vase. One you are fully engaged with visualizing that object, began to imagine moving toward it. Imagine your astral body floating, as it disengages from its physical self.

You may be able to look down and see your body. But if you can't, don't worry. Keep focusing on the feeling of floating and imagine yourself moving toward that vase.

The Rope Technique

This method was developed by a famous expert on astral projection named Robert Bruce. It focuses more on your senses than visualizing.

This imaginary rope is the main focal point in this method.

Keep your eyes closed and imagine a thick rope tied from your ceiling. It could be like the kind from a gym class. Maybe you've climbed one in real life, or maybe you've seen one climbed in a movie.

Just like with the visualization technique, you will feel and hear vibrations.

Once you feel ready, imagine yourself reaching up and grabbing the rope with your astral hand. Keep your eyes closed. Your physical hand should stay beside you on the bed. Once you've got one hand closed around the rope, imagine your other one coming up to join it.

Imagine that you are using your astral hands to pull yourself up from your body.

You may feel alarmed once you feel yourself start to separate from your body. This is normal. Take a deep breath and keep going. You may also feel like you can't move. Your body might feel paralyzed. Some people panic at this point and open their eyes or let go of the rope. If you do that, it's okay; you can try again.

Be aware these things may happen, and then keep going. Hold onto the rope, and imagine your entire body separating. Begin to climb the rope. Don't stop climbing until you are fully separate from your physical body.

For people who cannot imagine climbing a rope in real life and might find it overwhelming to pull themselves up, a ladder has been suggested by other experts, so that you can imagine using both your arms and your legs to propel yourself upward.

The Falling or Roll Out methods

These techniques are similar in that they involve imagining a physical action.

For the falling method, once you're in that vibrational state, think about how you're lying flat, and how your body is arranged on the bed. Be aware of how it feels.

Now imagine yourself free falling through the bed, down through the floor, and through the ground itself. With the roll out method, you'll roll out of your body, just as you roll out of bed. You'll turn or twist your astral body, just as you would if you were moving your physical body.

The Tunnel Method

Many of us will be familiar with this image. Most of us have probably heard the phrase, 'light at the end of the tunnel' to describe the feeling of hope when we think a difficult situation will soon be over.

People who have a near death experience often describe an experience where they travel through a tunnel, while also feeling drawn toward a bright light that's shining in the far distance. This idea is usually depicted as a dark rounded tunnel, much like an underground train tunnel, with a bright yellow light glowing at the end.

Imagine yourself in that underground tunnel. All around you are dark brick walls. But in front of you, there's a warm light. That light is where you want to reach.

Take slow steps at first, working your way toward the light. As the light gets closer, you may want to walk faster. Once you're comfortable walking quickly, start running. Then you'll progress into flying or floating.

5. Returning to your body

Once you've come back from a successful projection, you will likely have a heightened sense of awareness. Take some time to relax and think about your experience.

6. Journaling

Just as many experts recommend recording your dreams, many practitioners of astral travel recommend recording your experiences. Writing down how you feel and what you experienced is a valuable tool. It will also serve as a great way to document your progress.

Reminder: as important as the techniques we've explored so far in this chapter can be, the most important aspect is your own mindset and attitude. Believing in your spiritual self will take you much farther than getting every single step right.

What's it like?

While still connected to their physical body, some people have reported a warm flush that comes over their body, just as they move into the astral plane. Others have said they became chilled. Some feel their body get heavier, some feel their body get lighter. As we said at the start of this book, you are unique and so your experience of astral traveling will be unique to you too!

Despite the measured breathing and calm mind you used to get ready for astral projection, once you start you may experience a rapid heartbeat or a fast pulse. Your breathing may speed up too.

At this point, a few people experience sleep paralysis, where they're unable to move. It may feel alarming at first, but it's common so don't panic!

Don't be alarmed - it's actually a sign that your body is in a dream-like state, and astral projection may be imminent. And it will resolve as soon as you decide to end the astral travel attempt.

Once you're in the astral world, your bedroom, or the environment around your physical body should look the same. It won't look like an alien planet as soon as you leave your body.

Your astral body cannot move physical objects, but it can go through them. So, if you come to your front door and want to go outside, you can simply float through the door.

You may see streaks of light, or balls of colorful light that represent positive energy on the astral plane.

There's no gravity in the astral world though, so you can make your body do whatever you would like. You can walk, run, float, or fly. Your mind creates what it is that you can do. The only restrictions are the ones your mind creates.

Silver cord

When you enter the astral plane, you may see what looks like a silver cord linking your astral body to your physical form. This is the connection between our spirit and the material world. If you don't see it, don't worry. You're still connected to your body.

Even after these reassurances, if you still feel hesitant about leaving your body behind, practice visualizing what it will look like when you project before you try it for real.

Imagine a transparent version of yourself rising up and separating from your physical body. Once you've got that down, imagine that astral self turning around and looking at your physical body.

Astral travel allows us to see the world from an entirely different perspective. Once you can consistently make it out of your body, start your projection travels with a specific location in mind, don't plan to just wander.

And then, if you're wanting to connect to a spirit guide, you can focus on that as your goal.

Once you're more experienced, you can be a little more flexible in your planning.

Chapter Summary

- In this chapter we learned the step-by-step process to achieve your first astral projection.

- We learned too that there are several different methods of 'getting there'. Every person is different, and if one method doesn't work, then try another. Patience is a must when trying to find what method works for you.

- In the next chapter you will learn how to stay safe while practicing astral projection.

Chapter Six: How to Stay Safe while Trying Astral Projection

Physical preparation

Your astral body cannot be harmed while it's on the astral plane. It can't be injured or damaged.

However, your physical body can still be harmed. That's why it is crucial to find a place where your physical body is safe while you're projecting. A public library couch, or a grassy spot in a public park might feel relaxing, but it is important to find a place where you won't be disturbed by strangers.

It may be tempting to try it during a long meeting, or a boring school lecture, but please don't - you will only cause alarm to other people who'll likely think you're unconscious!

Also, don't try using drugs or other stimulants to induce your first astral travel. Yes, other people and even entire groups of people will have used them in the past with success, but it can be dangerous - even deadly. An open, calm, and prepared mind is the best and safest way to prepare for your astral journey.

Mental preparation

While it's true that achieving a calm mind is a big task, it's important to try before attempting to project. If your mind is overwhelmed with worry or by negative thoughts, you could end up panicking while you're projecting. The last thing you want to do while practicing astral travel is to increase your anxiety levels.

If it helps to think of astral projection as a form of self help, then do that.

You can also try positive affirmations if you're experiencing doubt about your ability to project. Come up with a phrase about how you're not afraid to visit the astral plane, or how you just know you'll be able to do it. Or even how you won't be scared while you're projecting. Once you've come up with your phrase, say it out loud.

Avoid dissociation

Dissociation can feel like we're not quite in our body, or as if we're entirely numb to what's going on around us. And instead of being a positive experience, it's often a response to a traumatic event, or even a stressful situation.

Dissociation is usually not a choice. It's something our brain does automatically for us, and it happens to protect us.

It's not recommended to use astral projection to avoid a problem. Seeking clarity on a problem, yes. But avoidance is not recommended.

Meditation

We addressed meditation in chapter four. If you haven't read that section yet, it's worth studying, as meditation is another ancient and safe practice that has helped millions of people gain access to the astral world.

Increase your mindfulness

Mindfulness means we are fully present in our lives, and that we are purposefully paying attention to our thoughts, our feelings, and our senses. We take note of our emotions, and what happens to us throughout the day.

You may learn a lot about yourself while you're projecting. You may also find it pretty overwhelming. If that happens, try to relax. Listen to some music, or call a trusted friend with whom you have discussed your plan to learn astral projection. Take note of what's going on around you in the real world.

Being mindful of what you're doing throughout the day can increase your comfort level when it's time to project.

When you're in the physical world, take note of what things feel like and smell like. Then start making the same observations in the astral world. This will help your mind process the differences in your two realities, and it will also help you identify time spent in a lucid dream, which we'll talk about later in the book in chapter nine.

Gratitude

Gratitude can help increase mindfulness. It's also one of the simplest ways to improve our mental health. Here are some ways to step up our gratitude.

Don't wait for something big to happen, like getting a promotion at work, or winning the lottery. We can start becoming more grateful by noticing small things, such as the taste of fresh pineapple for breakfast, a beautiful flower in bloom, or someone who is thoughtful enough to call us back when they said they would.

Start being aware of how thankful you are when good things happen. Each time you say the words 'thank you', stop for a minute and think about them. Don't just say them and move on to the next interaction. Also, become more aware of the people in your life, and what they do for you. And finally, acknowledge all of the good things you've received in your life so far.

As well as boosting mental health, practicing gratitude can also improve our immune system and our whole physical health. Ultimately, it will improve your astral projection practice as well!

As you become more comfortable with projection, you may start to see part of the astral world seep into your physical reality. These appearances could come in the form of distant voices, flashes of light, or a gentle ringing in your ears. Don't be alarmed by these occurrences. If they bother you, say out loud that you want them to stop, and they will.

However, try to see any crossover effects that you do experience as a positive signal that you're in tune with the astral world.

Chapter Summary

- In this chapter, we learned that astral travel is a safe activity.

- We discovered that practices such as mindfulness and gratitude can improve the experience of astral projection.

- In the next chapter you will learn what to do if you're having trouble projecting.

Chapter Seven: What to Do if You're Having Trouble Projecting

If you're having trouble, it's easy to get frustrated and give up. Some people project on the first try. But for some of us, it can take days, weeks, or months. Many experts have said that it took them almost a month of consistent practice to have any success at all. So, the important thing is to keep trying!

That said, there may be a few concrete reasons which explain why you might be struggling, and so we'll go through those possibilities and discover what to do about them.

Common problems may include:

1. Falling asleep

If you're falling asleep, you may need to choose a different spot to astral travel from - that you don't associate with sleeping. Try leaving your normal bed, and lying on the floor, or on a couch.

Some practitioners advise sleeping since you are clearly tired and then trying again when you're more awake.

2. A frantically racing mind

In the modern world, many of us spend the entire day stimulated thanks to phone calls, texts and emails, video conferences, and commutes in cars or trains. We may spend our evenings grocery shopping, cleaning our homes, cooking meals for our families, or looking after our kids. Many of us have a very long to-do list!

We need to learn how to set those frantic thoughts aside in order to be able to focus on quieting our mind.

That may feel as if we are being selfish or it may feel like we should be using that free time to do something else, like scrub the bathroom or pay bills online, but the benefits you'll acquire through astral travel will be worth the time you invest.

If you can't get your thoughts to stop, and you're not ready for meditation, try writing down every single thing you're thinking about on a piece of paper. Once you've had the chance to let it all out, then your mind should be ready to focus.

If that's not effective, try repeating a single word to yourself. You could even chant the sacred '*om*' sound which you learned about in chapter three.

3. Shallow breathing

Breathing seems pretty basic, and not least because it's something we do automatically and probably rarely stop to think about.

This may not seem like a big deal, but how we breathe when we prepare to go astral traveling can make or break our attempts! If you need a reminder on how to breathe correctly for the purposes of calming your mind to visit the astral plane, revisit chapter four, under the heading 'deep breathing.'

4. Fear of the astral world

These fears are valid, but once addressed, you can easily move past them.

Many people want to travel on the astral plane, but they're scared. That makes sense because it's an unfamiliar place to us. It's not something that's talked about in most workplaces, in school classrooms, or even among friends.

Our physical world is familiar - we spend all our waking hours there. But we can get familiar with the astral world even before we try to project there; by reading about it, by imagining it, and by practicing the techniques shared in this book. It just requires patience.

Some people are understandably afraid that once they're projected their body will stay separated from their mind, and they'll be trapped forever on the astral plane while their physical body remains unconscious.

Although this is something that's been shown in movies, this is not how projection works in real life. This cannot happen; you will always be linked to your body. And thankfully, there are no reports of anyone ever being stuck outside their body while voluntarily projecting.

Astral projection has been practiced by humans for thousands of years, and so if it were dangerous, or possible for our spirit to get stuck outside our body, then we'd know about it. The practitioners from thousands of years ago would have passed along strict warnings along with their stories.

While traveling, all you have to do is think about returning to your body, and it will happen instantly.

5. Feeling insecure in the time or location you've chosen

If you're worried about the alarm going off, or the baby waking up, or the dog scratching at the door, then all of these normal, everyday events can feel like an intrusion.

Some of our lives are more complicated than others. We may be caring for young children, or for an adult that needs our help. If that's the case, the only realistic time to project may be when they're sound asleep. Remember, not being disturbed is crucial to our success with astral travel.

6. Social conditioning

Some of us have been told that astral projection is the work of the devil, or that demons will possess us if we try it. Some religious leaders have told their constituents that astral projection dishonors God.

In truth, astral projection is not that different from dreams or daydreams. It doesn't seem likely that anyone would tell you that those are demonic!

You may have heard that malicious spirits will try to take over our body while you're traveling but that's simply not possible either. If you aren't afraid that evil spirits will take over your body while you're sleeping, then there's no reason to worry that they'll try to take over your body while you're involved in astral projection.

7. Being told it's not scientific

Whenever we're excited about a positive event or something new in our lives, we're all eager to share that excitement with our friends, coworkers, and family members. We want to share what we've learned, so that they can enjoy the benefits too.

But be aware - some people will not react well to your tales of astral traveling.

They may be dismissive. They may be rude. Sometimes they'll ridicule you, or astral travel itself. They may say you're gullible. They may cite a lack of hard data and say there's no scientific proof that anyone can have an OBE. They may warn you of the dangers, and claim you're being conned. The doubters may tell you that you shouldn't trust anyone who says they can project at all!

At first, you may feel crushed by all the negative comments. But just try to keep in mind that your friend/family member/work colleague doesn't have all the information you now have. He or she hasn't studied astral travel like you have.

Be patient. Don't force the topic. Eventually, the people who care about you may start to notice the positive changes you've made in your life thanks to astral projection, and they may start to come to you for advice.

Once they're ready, then you can point them in the right direction!

8. Expecting progress too quickly

There is no competition to see who can get to the astral plane first. At least, there shouldn't be! Each journey is a process. So don't feel like your process is happening too slowly. Expect that it will take a few weeks at least, just to get a feel for something you are new to and only just learning about.

9. Sporadic practice

As with any new undertaking and skill, practice is important. But the practice needs to be consistent. Just as weightlifters need to lift weights every week, astral travelers need a planned schedule as well. Pick a day or time that you'll practice and make a commitment to stick to that time slot.

Chapter Summary

- In this chapter we've explored many of the issues that might crop up and interfere with a successful astral projection practice.

- For each of those issues, we've discovered there are simple solutions to get you back on the right track.

- In the next chapter you will learn what to do after you've successfully visited the astral plane.

Chapter Eight: What happens next? Expanding on what you've learned

Once you've conquered the hard part, which is actually getting out of your body, you may wonder what happens next?

In some ways, that's up to you.

The astral world is a dynamic place, just as the physical world is. Focus on how thrilled you are to have finally made it to the astral plane. You will probably feel far more emotional there than you do in the physical world. And that's okay. Just let those feelings happen.

This is a place that's governed by thoughts, not rules, and you get to shape your own experiences by setting your goals and intent before you project.

Where do you want to go? Do you want to travel to a physical location on the earth, such a favorite mountain or hiking trail? If so, do what we have learned and focus solely on that place.

Picture what that place was like for you when you visited it in the physical world. Did you enjoy the sound of the rushing water in a nearby stream? Did you like the smell of the pine trees? Focus on all of those sensory points.

If the place you want to visit is in the past, that's possible too. Picture the same details from that moment in the past as vividly as possible.

If you want to fly, imagine yourself looking down at the tops of the trees. If you prefer the ocean, imagine yourself skimming over the tops of the waves, or diving deep into the sea.

There are no limits - except those you set for yourself!

Visiting with the deceased

For the visit to work, the other person who has departed the physical plane must be interested in meeting you again too. If there was unresolved tension between the two of you when they passed away, it may take some time for them to agree to meet with you.

The best mindset for visiting the deceased is one of love and acceptance. And it is actively discouraged for you to ask the deceased person to guide you in your physical life on earth - that's a mindset that can only hamper you and will hold them back from their higher pursuits now they are no longer walking the earth.

To locate the person you're looking for, look at a photo of them before you begin your astral projection session, or hold something in your hands that belonged to them. Sometimes, you will find your loved one already waiting for you; sometimes you may have to spend more time looking. They will often come to you when you're ready.

Also, keep in mind, that the deceased person you are visiting may not look exactly as you remember them - they will have chosen the form that now feels most appropriate to them.

Spirit Guides

Once you're comfortable in traveling to and around the astral plane, you may want to look for a guide. These are 'beings' that have transitioned out of a physical body and now live in the astral plane permanently. Astral experts say you can simply ask for one, and sometimes, a guide will just appear.

Your guide may be someone you knew in life, or it may be a higher being.

Our guides want to help us to become our best selves. They are beings who've mastered a certain level of spiritual competence, and they've volunteered to help the living with their struggles. Each of us may have multiple guides, but that we all have at least one who will be with us throughout our life in the physical world, from cradle to grave.

We can ask our spirit guides for help with anything, big or small. Divorce, health issues, or work problems are all concerns we can take directly to our spirit guide. Or if we have a spiritual question that we need answered, they are always willing to help nurture us on that path too.

Meeting with beings from outer space

If it's possible for any of us to travel the earth while on the astral plane, then why not travel to other planets?

In 1774, a Swedish philosopher named Emanuel Swedenborg wrote about his astral experiences. He detailed his journey to the Moon, and on to Mars, Mercury, Saturn, Venus, and Jupiter. Since then, others have described their journeys to celestial bodies and other worlds. Two well-known more contemporary astral travelers, Robert Bruce and Robert Monroe claim to have traveled to outer space.

The next few topics are not a formal part of astral travel, but they are related. Awareness of these concepts can help you on your path to becoming more enlightened.

Time travel

According to astral experts, time does not exist in the astral world. That means it's possible to travel into the past, and even to visit events and people we've only heard about in history books. This will not come easily as a beginner, but it is possible later on in your journey.

Reincarnation

Reincarnation is the idea that when a person dies, his or her soul is reborn, and goes on to inhabit the body of a newborn baby.

Reincarnation is a central tenant in Hinduism, Sikhism, Jainism, and Buddhism. In Sikhism, for example, a major religion in India, a person, or a soul, remains in the cycle of reincarnation until he or she becomes one with God.

But in other religions, such as Christianity, Judaism, and Islam, most of the followers believe a human has one life, and then moves on to the afterlife.

Some experts believe reincarnation is the reason why humans and their qualities can be so vastly different from one another. Some souls appear to be much further evolved than others. The explanation would be that the ones we refer to as 'old souls' have lived many lives before, and that the ones who are immature have not.

Psychiatrist Ian Stevenson was an avid researcher of the idea of reincarnation. In his lab at the University of Virginia, he studied OBEs, near death experiences, apparitions, deathbed visions, and children who remembered former lives.

He studied young children, aged two to five, who had unexplained phobias or detailed memories of former lives. Sometimes he had remarkable findings, such as children who could corroborate details they should otherwise not have known.

During his forty years of research, he studied 2,500 cases of potential reincarnation and published four books.

His research wasn't accepted by the scientific community, but it was invaluable to those who know there's more to us than our physical bodies, and to those who are interested in exploring the spiritual and psychic possibilities that extend beyond anything we can currently prove in a lab.

Karma

Karma is a key principle in Hinduism, and it relates to reincarnation. Karma is based on the idea that there is a kind of spiritual cause and effect. With karma, the belief is that good acts will lead to good outcomes for a soul, and that bad acts will lead to a poor outcome. When the person is reincarnated, his or her current life situation is thought to be based on the behaviors he or she chose in a past life.

Past Life Regressions

If you find yourself wanting to explore your past lives, astral projection is a significant way to help accomplish that goal. And if you need assistance, there are specific forms of hypnosis therapy that help us to discover and address our past lives.

During a past life regression with a trained therapist, a person is said to be able to recall their past lives.

There are benefits to this that go beyond enlightenment. There are, for instance, some people who have unexplained chronic illness, or phobias that developed with no explanation.

The idea here is that we can heal ourselves by finding out what happened to us in a past life. Once we know the origins of our pain, whether it's mental, physical, or spiritual, we can begin to work through it.

Ascension

Ascension can happen when light and energy from other realms enters your body.

The symptoms include headaches, a ringing in the ears, and an increase in synchronicities.

Ascension and its symptoms are not something to be afraid of. They happen naturally, as your body adjusts to the higher frequencies of the astral plane.

Synchronicities

Renowned Swiss doctor and psychoanalyst Carl Jung defined synchronicities as "meaningful coincidences".

They can show up as numbers, names or patterns and tend to crop up over and over until they have your attention. We always have these occurrences in our lives, but ascension increases their frequency.

Once you're further into your astral projection journey, you may start to notice all the coincidences in your life. They may have already been there, but you weren't quite aware enough to notice them, or they may actually start to increase as you open up your mind.

An example would be that you're thinking about a friend whom you haven't seen in a year, and then a song comes on that radio that features her name, and then your phone rings - and yes, it's that friend calling you to catch up.

Synchronicities and coincidences can come in any form: people, numbers, patterns, dreams, objects, and events. We just have to be more tuned in to our minds, as well as the world around us, to notice them.

Just like dream journaling, the process of recording these magical occurrences will help you focus your mind on all the meaningful connections in your life, and seeing them all written down will show you just how common they are.

As always, keep pursuing astral projection, and you'll find yourself more adept at seeing your coincidences, and realize you are more in tune with the universe than ever.

Furthering your studies

You may find yourself with a deep longing for more information about astral projection at some point during your journey. Sometimes, we don't know anyone in our own lives who is interested and so you may wish to build relationships with new friends and like-minded people who see the value in visiting the astral world.

Happily, there are plenty of great places to meet, both in person and online to hang out with people who want to discuss the astral world.

Robert Monroe Institute

Robert Monroe began his journey with astral projection in the 1950s, after an accidental OBE. After years of research, he founded the Institute in the early 1970s, to further research and educate people on the topic of astral projection.

The Institute is in Virginia, in the United States. It offers dozens of classes on the campus, and also online. They also offer retreats. Most of all, the participants consider themselves a community, which is often appealing to a lot of practitioners.

Besides that Institute, there are hundreds of other experienced practitioners who offer classes. There are podcasts, videos, books, and websites all dedicated to astral travel.

Of course, you don't have to pay for a class or travel to take a retreat. There are resources everywhere. If you can't find a local group of interested people, you could try starting your own group.

Chakras

The concept of chakras is also an ancient one. They are based on the idea that we have these distinct but invisible energy centers in our bodies.

The word chakra means 'whirling ball' in Sanskrit. There are seven chakras in the body, and they control the flow of energy through our physical selves. Sometimes they can be blocked, which then hampers the flow of energy. But when all of them are open, our body, mind, and spirit operate in harmony, with all parts working together.

The seven chakras are: the crown chakra, the third eye chakra, the throat chakra, the heart chakra, the solar plexus chakra, the sacral chakra, and the root chakra.

The Third Eye chakra

You may have already heard of the 'Third Eye.' What this refers to is the 'mind's eye', or the 'inner eye', which is the chakra located in the center of your forehead.

The Third Eye allows us to see beyond the more mundane aspects to who we really are. It's linked to clairvoyance and intuition, and allows us to understand those aspects of life that are beyond the typical human experience, such as astral travel, and how our consciousness can expand and move beyond our physical body.

Opening our Third Eye allows us to see ourselves more fully. We can view our strengths and weaknesses with objectivity.

What happens when the third eye chakra is blocked?

Any of the seven chakras can get blocked, which can lead to illness both physically and spiritually. Each chakra has a direct relationship to our physical body.

The Third Eye chakra is connected to the pituitary gland, which regulates the endocrine (hormone) system. This imbalance can cause many issues if not dealt with. If your Third Eye is blocked, you may experience sinus problems, headaches, hormone imbalances, eye strain, or mood issues.

There are a number of steps you can follow to begin awakening and unblocking your third eye.

The first thing you can do, is to start journaling. In the journal, you write down all the factual statements about yourself, such as, 'I am a sister,' or 'I am a seamstress.' Then imagine yourself ten years in the future and write a similar list for your future self. Then pick a point in the past and do the same thing. After you're done, compare the lists, and think about how you see yourself; you can then also analyze how your sense of self has changed over the years.

The second is 'acting', by using our emotions. Because our emotions are so strongly connected to how we behave, and how we perceive ourselves.

Start by picking an emotion tied to a memory, and then practice feeling that emotion in the present moment. If we choose joy, we could pick a happy memory, and then make ourselves smile and laugh. If we pick a sad memory, we make ourselves cry. If we pick rage, we can act that out by screaming. Don't allow the emotions to stay with you very long; move through each one as an exercise.

The third step is to keep a dream journal. The more you can tap into the memories of your dreams, the better your relationship will be with your unconscious mind. Write down everything you can remember about your dreams, and if you find that you can't remember your dream, spend a few minutes meditating before getting up. With practice, you will start to remember.

Auras

All of us have an aura that surrounds our physical body. It's made up of an electromagnetic energy field, and whilst invisible to most people, those with psychic and healing abilities can see this colored 'field' around other people.

Our auras are affected by our mental state, and they are always changing. Some experts believe these changes reflect what's going on with our spirit. So, when we're encountering setbacks, or we're in a negative headspace, our aura is affected. Conversely, when we're doing well and pursuing enlightenment, our aura is bright and radiant.

Astral travel and other practices mentioned in this book, such as meditation, deep breathing, and yoga can all improve the state of anyone's aura.

Other ways to heal our auras include being out in nature, exercise, a healthy diet of fruits and vegetables, essential oils, good sleep, and color healing. As with astral projection, visualization can further help us cleanse our aura.

To do this, imagine your aura surrounding your body. Then imagine cleaning it with positive energy, erasing the negative energies that are weighing you down.

We can also use crystals to help heal our aura - we'll talk about using crystals in the next section.

Humans are not the only beings with auras. Every living thing has an aura, including animals, trees, and plants. One of the easier auras to view is that of a tree.

If you'd like to view your own aura, there are methods to achieve that. Begin by holding your hand up in front of a white wall. Focus on the space between your fingers. As you continue to look between your fingers, you will eventually see a fuzzy looking glow emanating from your fingers. That's your aura! Once you've practiced, you may start to see colors.

Once you feel confident spotting the aura around your hand, try looking in the mirror to see more of your own aura. You will also be able to see the auras of other people too, by first looking right past them, and not focusing on their physical self. Once you've practiced long enough, you may see auras without trying.

Crystals

If you want something tangible to hold while you're attempting to clear your mind, crystals are a good choice.

You can buy a crystal in a store or online, or if you're in a place where it's permitted, you can find your own in nature. There are crystal mines in some locations where you can dig for your own for a small fee.

Crystals are said to have and to hold vibrational healing energy. Each one of them has a different vibrational energy, and so just holding one in your hand can have a positive effect. Don't think of the crystals as being just a rock, but as a dynamic part of the earth that holds energy. You can then create your own relationship with each one you use.

But, if you want to intentionally program the crystals with a specific energy, then you'll get an even bigger benefit.

Outside of meditation, crystals have been used for thousands of years for healing and for protection.

When you first get the crystal, cleanse it. This can be done with moonlight or sunlight, by letting it sit out overnight, or during the day. If you want to cleanse it faster, use salt and water in a small basin.

Once it's cleansed, you can 'program' it. There's no exact way to do it; so, you may want to experiment and see what works for you.

This can be done by getting familiar with your crystal. Hold it, look at it, observe how it feels. Breathe deeply and visualize sending your energy into the crystal. Then imagine the crystal helping you achieve what it is that you need, such as a successful astral projection. Imagine yourself lying down, and then picture your astral body leaving the physical plane. Or you can speak directly to your crystal.

You can say to it, 'I would like you to help me with my journey into the astral plane." Describe what it is that you would like to do, with specific requests. Say the words out loud, and repeat them. Once you've programmed your crystals, carry them with you all the time.

Color therapy

Color therapy is an alternative healing method. Like astral projection, it's been around for thousands of years, and was even documented in ancient Egypt.

It uses colors to promote mental, physical, and spiritual healing in the human body. Each color has its own energy output and can be used to rebalance the chakras. Indigo is the color recommended for balancing the third eye chakra, and that's the color most closely connected to our astral projection journey.

If you'd like to explore color therapy more, there are therapists who use it as a form of treatment, and you can find more specific guidance online and try it for yourself. As with other types of healing outlined in this book, it should not be used in place of medical advice.

Chapter Summary

- In this chapter, we touched on some more advanced concepts such as chakras, reincarnation, and crystals.

- As with astral projection, all of these concepts require an open mind, but if you are able to embrace them, then they will only enhance your astral travel practice.

- In the next chapter you will learn about lucid dreams.

Chapter Nine: Lucid Dreaming

We've devoted an entire chapter to dreaming, because although it's usually not an intentional form of an OBE, dreaming is related to the practice of astral travel with some people using dreams as a gateway to astral projection.

First, though, we need to change the way we think about our dreams. Begin to treat your dreams as an important resource on your path to becoming an astral traveler; and see them as a gateway to understanding lucid dreaming and astral projection.

Lucid Dreaming

This is the name of a type of dream that is intentional.

Lucid dreams are in the same family as astral projections, but they are not actually projections, because the environment is still your dream world, and your body is asleep, even if your mind is awake.

With astral projection, your body and mind are both awake.

But lucid dreams are different from regular dreams because you *know* you're dreaming while it's happening - you're aware, and you're controlling what happens.

Like many of the other concepts mentioned in this book, lucid dreaming is no longer considered a fringe idea. It's been used by therapists to treat PTSD, night terrors, or extreme anxiety. Sometimes it happens with no effort. But many of us can learn to control it and use it at will.

Some people have found lucid dreaming easier to master than astral travel, and use it as a precursor to visiting the astral world.

If we come to view sleep as another state of consciousness to be explored, it will help us with our astral projection journey. For this to happen, we have to think about our dreams differently and not as something passive that happens to us, but as something that we're in charge of.

Wake Back to Bed (WBTB)

A popular method for lucid dreams is called the Wake Back to Bed method. For this method, you set an alarm five hours after you go to bed. Then you go to sleep as you normally would.

When the alarm goes off, you get up. You stay up for thirty minutes, and do something relaxing, like read. Then after the thirty-minute mark, you go back to sleep again.

Once you've gone back to sleep, you're much more likely to be able to engage in lucid dreaming.

Reality Testing Method

Another method commonly practiced is Reality Testing. It's the best way to test your self-awareness. Too often, when we're in the dream state, we feel like we're in the real world.

It is recommended to try to push the fingers of one hand through the palm of your other hand. In the physical world, obviously your fingers won't go through your hand. But while you're dreaming, they often will.

There are other good real-world reasons to learn lucid dreaming. Some veterans have found relief from PTSD after mastering lucid dreaming, and there are athletes who have used the skill to improve their sports performance.

The improvement of sports performance is based on the idea that practicing a difficult athletic maneuver in the dream state can improve its success in the physical world. It's a great way to try out a challenging new skill within the safety of a dream and can help injured athletes to practice while they're recovering. It's also thought to give athletes a good way to visualize their success on the day of a game or competition.

In addition, people who frequently suffered from frequent nightmares found the frequency of their nightmares decreased after they learned the skill of lucid dreaming.

With practice, you'll learn to control the dream world. Once your mind has expanded to include lucid dreaming, your astral projections will only become more enriching.

Chapter Summary

- In this chapter, we learned about lucid dreaming, and how it relates to astral projections, as well as methods to help us learn to awaken ourselves into a lucid state while dreaming.
- We also learned a few reasons why anyone would want to master the skill of lucid dreaming.

Final Words

It's true that there's a lot of information to digest in this book, but all of it is within your reach.

Remember, that while astral projection may sound easy, it is truly a learned skill that takes a lot of time and energy to master.

This guide has shown you how astral projection is useful and how it's used, and you've been given a step-by-step beginner's guide for how to actually start your practice of traveling safely to the astral plane.

If you get stuck, remember to keep trying. And if you need them, there are several options listed in this book for you to try to get yourself back on track.

Keep trying - practice every chance you get. It will get easier, and then it will become something you look forward to each day.

If you continue to devote time and energy to your practice, soon you will reach a new form of enlightenment. Before you know it, you'll be able to project yourself into a world most people can only imagine or dream of visiting!

www.ingramcontent.com/pod-product-compliance
Lightning Source LLC
LaVergne TN
LVHW021736060526
838200LV00052B/3304